Too Many

Things
to Tie Up

TWO DOZEN OR SO SILLY POEMS FOR KIDS

Written By: H.A. Harper
Illustrated by: Riley Norris

Inkwell and Pen, LLC

DEDICATED TO DAD

THANKS FOR HELPING ALONG THE WAY.

-HARP

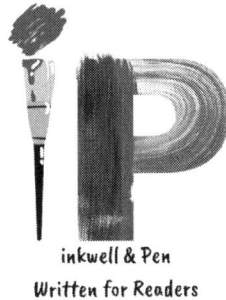

inkwell & Pen
Written for Readers

www.inkwellandpenllc.com

For contact:

inkwellandpenllc@gmail.com

FOLLOW US ON INSTAGRAM @HAHARPER_AUTHOR

(Insert Intro Here)

Did you know
you are about to read
the poems of
an eight year old?
Well, mostly that is the case.
I will not lie!
She got some help from her father
who is, in his heart,
eight
(though he is actually thirty-five).

I guess that counts, just fine.

Too Many Things to Tie Up

Too many things to tie up!
Too many things to tie up!
It's frightful to know there are
too many things to tie up.

(Especially when I've just refused
to tie a T-Rex's tennis shoes.)

Sideways Lilly

Sideways Lilly lived in a sideways house.
Her only friend was a sideways mouse.
Lilly and her mouse loved to sideways joust,
a dance you can dance in a sideways house.

One day Lilly stepped out of her house
with her little friend, Sideways Mouse.
They stepped out onto Rightways Hill
and began tumbling. What an awful spill!
But because her name was Sideways Lil',
she didn't fall the right way downhill.
Instead, she tumbled round and round.
Always going down...down...down...

So if you ever walk up Rightways Hill,
look out for little old Sideways Lil'.
And please pray for poor Sideways Mouse,
for he's forever rolling round Sideways House.

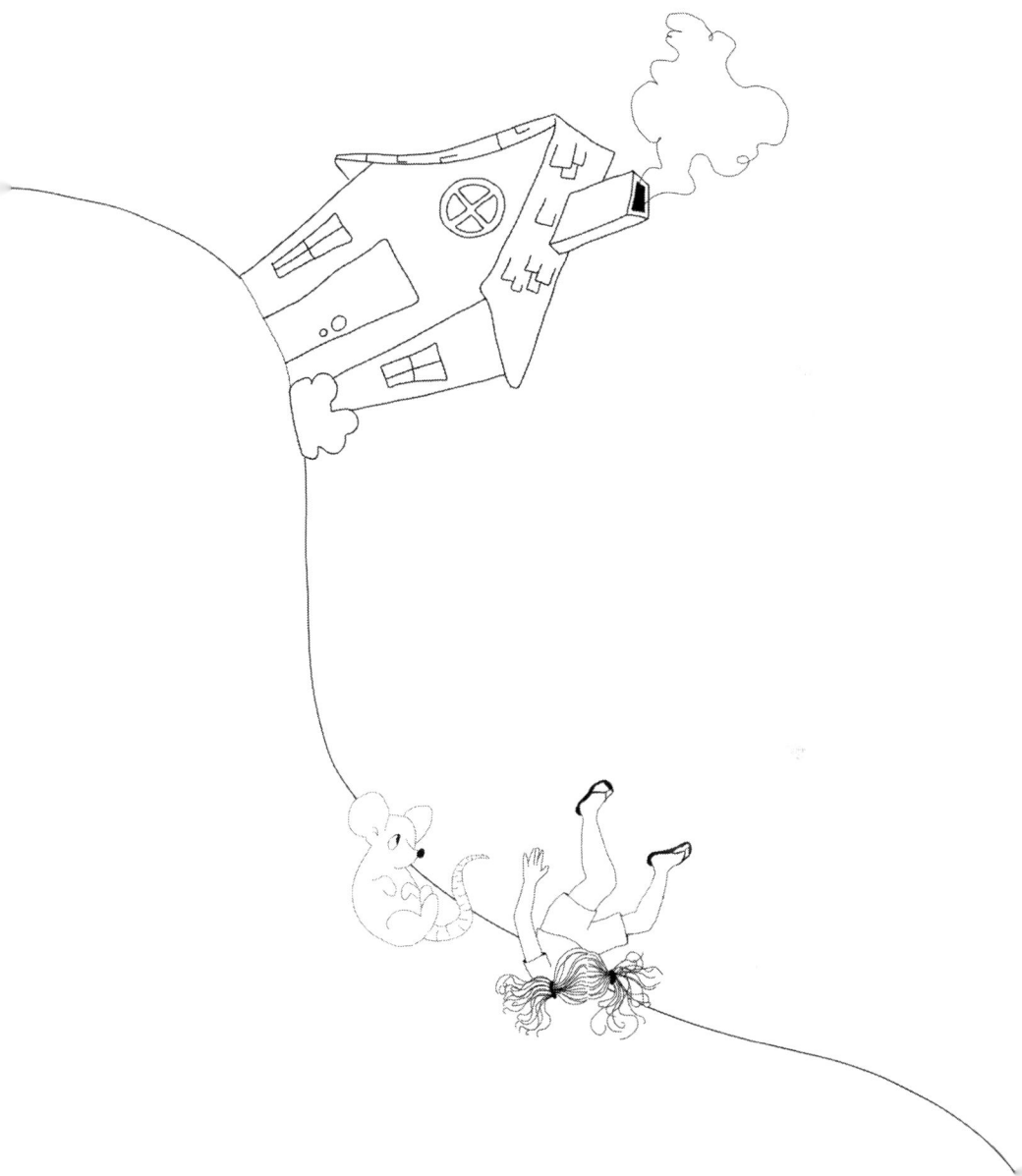

Memphis and I

While I was walking down the street,
without warning I
suddenly tripped over my feet.
I turned my eyes quickly to see
the cutest culprit staring back at me—

a very slick, very sly, but very sweet,
cute-as-a-button, pretty piebald puppy...
named Memphis.

Something's Cooking!

In a cave, deep in the dark woods
there was a shadow wearing a hood.
It was a witch with a warty nose,
slinky fingers, and (Whew!) smelly toes.

She hopped and twirled as she sung
a song that I thought was
(Oh!) so dumb.
These are the words
that the witch sung:

"By the pricking
of my
snail-slimed
thumb,
something's
cooking.
I hope it's
a sugar plum."

Gunk!

Close your mouth

and open your eyes,

so you don't get

a non-good surprise.

Playful Pups

Over the boat,
three playful pups float
through the sky,
just them and I.

Pooper Scooper!

Pooper scooper!
Pooper scooper!

How do you make a pooper scooper?

Take the one that
   does
   the
   pooping
and make him or her
   do
   all
   the
   scooping.

A Mischievous Toad

'Twas the night
after Christmas,
when all through the hills
the toads were all playing,
enjoying their spills.
But one little toad read
The Wind in the Willows,
'stead of playing leapfrog,
protected by pillows!

An Animal Party

An animal party! An animal party!
I can't believe
I'm throwing an animal party!

What music will we have?
What games will we play?
What will we eat?
What should the invitations say?

Oh! Oh! I've got it!

I know how they will read!

"Come one, come all
from land and sea,
come and join my friends and me
at the palace by the sea
and we will have an animal party.

Over, over by the sea
there lies an animal party
that will be thrown
by the one and only—
yours truly."

Barbecued Chili

"Barbecued Chili! Nice and hot!
Barbecued Chili! It hits the spot!"

"Who ordered
the Barbecued Chili?"

"I did, sir.
But I wanted
it fried."

A Shoey Culprit

One day while walking down the street,
without warning, I suddenly tripped over my feet.
When I reached to rub the pain from my knee,
I saw the culprit staring back at me.

Tongue out of its mouth and awfully aloof,
were the untied strings of my favorite tennis shoes.

Honey Buns

Have you ever seen
a bundle of busy bees
buzzing about your honey buns?

Well if you ever do,
  you better

RUN,

RUN,

RUN!

Billy Bop Boop's Problem

Billy Bop Boop from Zoopaloop
had a real problem, you see.

His zipper wouldn't come undone,
and so he screamed and screamed.

"Darn you, ZIPPER...!!!"

Then, twisting and hopping,
he began to run down the street,

"Help me! Help me! Help me!
My zipper is stuck.
Please,
help me get this thing undone!
It hurts!   It hurts!

I zipped up my thumb!"

Secret Potion

Dogfish tails and catfish whiskers.
Camel spider hair and spider monkey fingers.
Mix them in a bowl with dragon fruit jelly.
Swallow it down and swish it in your belly.

That's the secret potion
for getting out of chores,
but after you've done it once
you won't do it anymore.

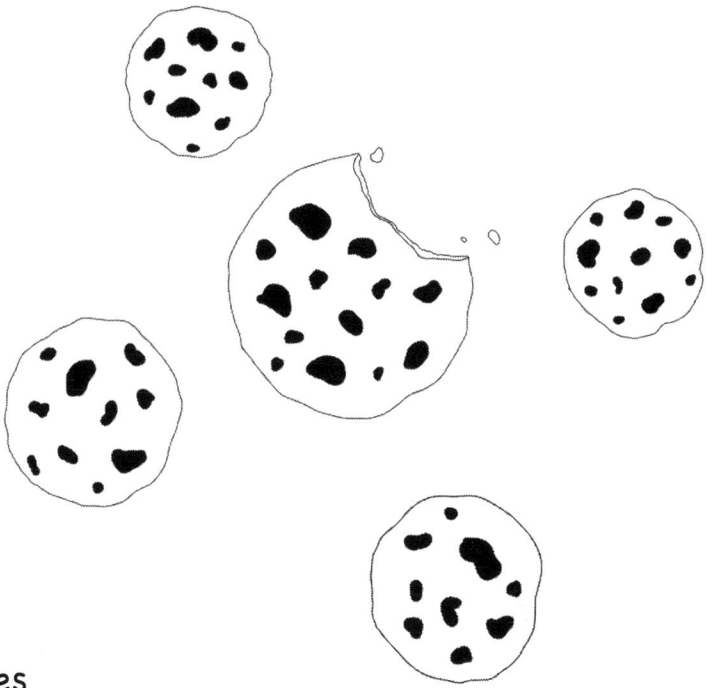

Cookies

Of all the crazy things
I've heard my parents say,
This one takes the cake.

"If a cookie a day
keeps the doctor away,
two is better for you."

So I never eat a cookie.
Instead, I eat two.

Mo Branson

Little Mo Branson (only 3 foot 3),
proud and loud and silly as can be,
was quite shockingly fleet of the feet.

No one his height could beat him in a heat.
When it came to sticking his tongue out,
Mo was the fastest draw in the south.

His favorite pastime?
Running his mouth
with insulting gibberish
only he could spit out.

Dance! Sing! Eat! Nap!

I love to dance with
my favorite arachnid!
I love to sing the blues
with earthworms in my shoes!
I love to eat fresh cake
with a slimy, slurpy snake!
I love to take a nap
with a raccoon on my back!

Somersault Sue

Somersault Sue,
we all love you,
but why do you
somersault all
day?

We'd like you
to run
andjump
and play,

but instead you
somersault all day.

They're Coming for Me!

Creak...Creak...Creak...
Something goes bump in the night.
Creak... Creak... Creak...
I pull up the sheets
Creak... Creak... Creak...
under my nose and open my eyes.
Creak... Creak... Creak...
I see them watching me,
Creak... Creak... Creak...
those eyes, in the cold, dead of night.
They hover and glow.

                    Creak... Creak... Creak...
                    Scratch...Scratch...Scratch...
                    Closer... Closer... Closer...
                    They're coming! They're coming!
                    Creak... Creak...Creak...
                    They're coming for me!
                    Creak... Creak... Creak...
                    I'm shivering in my sheets.
                    Creak... Creak... Creak...
                    My teeth chatter.
                    Creak...Creak...Creak...
                    My knees knock.

Creak... Creak... Creak...
I can hear them breathe.
Creak... Creak... Creak...
It whispers my name.

Creak... Creak... Creak...
Those eyes! Those eyes!
Those frightful eyes!!!
Click-click!
Then...
my mother turns on the light.

Poetic Soul

I pick up my pencil and squiggle and dot.
I write rhyming words that I hope are not rot.
I pour out my heart on blue-lined pages
thinking of lines I hope will not fade with
the strings of time as they become untied.
I cannot help but imagine my biggest rhymes
are really so little among the many things
that come and go in time and space.
Still, I will string together many words
for a laugh, for a smile each time they're heard.

That is enough for a simple poetic soul
to pass through this happy world...whole.

A Beautiful Day

The grass was light green.
The sky was dark blue.
All the puppies were playing
and the birds chirping, too.
The sun was warm, as it should be.
The wind was nice and cool,
blowing the leaves,
carrying a cloudless tune.

CRASH! SLAM! WHACK! POW!
    The thunder and lightning and rain
    came tumbling, tumbling, tumbling down.
    Oh, me. Oh, my. What can I say?
    And it was such a beautiful day.

Using Your Senses in the Outdoors

The birds are tweeting beautifully.
The wind is blowing softifully.
Some dark clouds are coming this wayfully.
There are a lot of treesfully.
The air smells nicefully.
I feel really coolfully.
The sky is bright bluefully.

Be Witched

I got thrown into a pot.
I sat upon a leprechaun.
What fun things to do
whenever you are new!

Bouncehouse Bobby

Bouncehouse Bobby was big, tough, and mean.
He growled and roared and gnashed his teeth.

With a flick of the wrist, he sent kids flying
out the door of his bounce house—running, crying.

One day Bobby made the wrong mommy mad.
(That mommy was tougher than Bouncehouse's dad.)

That mommy came growling and
      roaring and gnashing.
           Down on Bouncehouse's head,
               her wrath came crashing.

Then that mommy picked Bobby up to his feet,
dusted him off and said something sweet.

"Oh, dear Bobby," that tough mommy heeded,
"Use your strength where it's really needed.

Help the weak, the poor, and the needy.
Protect them from the bad, ugly, and greedy."

Then that mommy sent Bobby on his merry way
with a knot on his head that he still has today.

But Bobby never picked on another kid again.
Instead, he became all the little kids' friend.

He protected them from all the big, bad bullies,
for Bouncehouse Bobby was a true friend, truly.

Animals Need You

Even though some animals may scare you,
don't let them, because they might need you.
If you see or hear a hurt animal out in the
wild blue,
there is something that you can do.
Call a vet or zoologist to come and help you.
Not only do people need help, animals need
help, too.

The End of the World

The world was shaking
and people were trembling with fright,
for it was the end...
of the world!

...TO BE CONTINUED...

Made in the USA
Las Vegas, NV
10 December 2022

61188379R00022